BOOK WRITING
GUIDE & PLANNER

AUTHOR: _____

ISBN: 978-1-63616-109-9
Library of Congress Control Number: 2018941255

Published, edited and illustrated by:
Opportune Independent Publishing Company

For permission requests, write to the publisher, addressed "Attention: Permissions Coordinator," at the address below.

info@opportunepublishing.com
www.opportunepublishing.com

CONTENTS

"
FIRST THINGS
FIRST,
WRITE!

—OPPORTUNE PUBLISHING

Hey Author!

The Book Writing Guide & Planner has been created for YOU! When you're ready to write your first (or next) book, but you just aren't sure how you're going to get through it. Use this as a resource to learn the steps to becoming an author and the things you should be thinking about along the way.

The No. 1 thing to do when writing a book is WRITE! It's extremely easy to get caught up in the idea, research, and hype of writing a book. Many people put pressure on themselves so much so that it removes the focus from the task at hand—Writing a book. No matter what, always simply continue to write your book. Don't worry about it being perfect, or think too far ahead. No matter what, it all begins with you removing the content and ideas from your head and putting it on paper. So throughout this process, WRITE, WRITE and WRITE!

OUTLINE 1

QUESTION(S) NEEDING TO BE ANSWERED

PURPOSE FOR WRITING THIS BOOK

PLOT

THINGS TO INCLUDE

OUTLINE 2

TITLE OF BOOK

PURPOSE OF WRITING BOOK

BOOK SUMMARY

CHARACTERS

CHAPTER TITLES

2022

January

Su	Mo	Tu	We	Th	Fr	Sa
26	27	28	29	30	31	1
2	3	4	5	6	7	8
9	10	11	12	13	14	15
16	17	18	19	20	21	22
23	24	25	26	27	28	29
30	31					

February

Su	Mo	Tu	We	Th	Fr	Sa
30	31	1	2	3	4	5
6	7	8	9	10	11	12
13	14	15	16	17	18	19
20	21	22	23	24	25	26
27	28					

March

Su	Mo	Tu	We	Th	Fr	Sa
27	28	1	2	3	4	5
6	7	8	9	10	11	12
13	14	15	16	17	18	19
20	21	22	23	24	25	26
27	28	29	30	31		

April

Su	Mo	Tu	We	Th	Fr	Sa
27	28	29	30	31	1	2
3	4	5	6	7	8	9
10	11	12	13	14	15	16
17	18	19	20	21	22	23
24	25	26	27	28	29	30

May

Su	Mo	Tu	We	Th	Fr	Sa
1	2	3	4	5	6	7
8	9	10	11	12	13	14
15	16	17	18	19	20	21
22	23	24	25	26	27	28
29	30	31				

June

Su	Mo	Tu	We	Th	Fr	Sa
29	30	31	1	2	3	4
5	6	7	8	9	10	11
12	13	14	15	16	17	18
19	20	21	22	23	24	25
26	27	28	29	30		

July

Su	Mo	Tu	We	Th	Fr	Sa
26	27	28	29	30	1	2
3	4	5	6	7	8	9
10	11	12	13	14	15	16
17	18	19	20	21	22	23
24	25	26	27	28	29	30
31						

August

Su	Mo	Tu	We	Th	Fr	Sa
31	1	2	3	4	5	6
7	8	9	10	11	12	13
14	15	16	17	18	19	20
21	22	23	24	25	26	27
28	29	30	31			

September

Su	Mo	Tu	We	Th	Fr	Sa
28	29	30	31	1	2	3
4	5	6	7	8	9	10
11	12	13	14	15	16	17
18	19	20	21	22	23	24
25	26	27	28	29	30	

October

Su	Mo	Tu	We	Th	Fr	Sa
25	26	27	28	29	30	1
2	3	4	5	6	7	8
9	10	11	12	13	14	15
16	17	18	19	20	21	22
23	24	25	26	27	28	29

November

Su	Mo	Tu	We	Th	Fr	Sa
30	31	1	2	3	4	5
6	7	8	9	10	11	12
13	14	15	16	17	18	19
20	21	22	23	24	25	26
27	28	29	30			

December

Su	Mo	Tu	We	Th	Fr	Sa
27	28	29	30	1	2	3
4	5	6	7	8	9	10
11	12	13	14	15	16	17
18	19	20	21	22	23	24
25	26	27	28	29	30	31

2023

January

Su	Mo	Tu	We	Th	Fr	Sa
1	2	3	4	5	6	7
8	9	10	11	12	13	14
15	16	17	18	19	20	21
22	23	24	25	26	27	28
29	30	31				

February

Su	Mo	Tu	We	Th	Fr	Sa
			1	2	3	4
5	6	7	8	9	10	11
12	13	14	15	16	17	18
19	20	21	22	23	24	25
26	27	28				

March

Su	Mo	Tu	We	Th	Fr	Sa
			1	2	3	4
5	6	7	8	9	10	11
12	13	14	15	16	17	18
19	20	21	22	23	24	25
26	27	28	29	30	31	

April

Su	Mo	Tu	We	Th	Fr	Sa
						1
2	3	4	5	6	7	8
9	10	11	12	13	14	15
16	17	18	19	20	21	22
23	24	25	26	27	28	29
30						

May

Su	Mo	Tu	We	Th	Fr	Sa
	1	2	3	4	5	6
7	8	9	10	11	12	13
14	15	16	17	18	19	20
21	22	23	24	25	26	27
28	29	30	31			

June

Su	Mo	Tu	We	Th	Fr	Sa
				1	2	3
4	5	6	7	8	9	10
11	12	13	14	15	16	17
18	19	20	21	22	23	24
25	26	27	28	29	30	

July

Su	Mo	Tu	We	Th	Fr	Sa
						1
2	3	4	5	6	7	8
9	10	11	12	13	14	15
16	17	18	19	20	21	22
23	24	25	26	27	28	29
30	31					

August

Su	Mo	Tu	We	Th	Fr	Sa
		1	2	3	4	5
6	7	8	9	10	11	12
13	14	15	16	17	18	19
20	21	22	23	24	25	26
27	28	29	30	31		

September

Su	Mo	Tu	We	Th	Fr	Sa
					1	2
3	4	5	6	7	8	9
10	11	12	13	14	15	16
17	18	19	20	21	22	23
24	25	26	27	28	29	30

October

Su	Mo	Tu	We	Th	Fr	Sa
1	2	3	4	5	6	7
8	9	10	11	12	13	14
15	16	17	18	19	20	21
22	23	24	25	26	27	28
29	30	31				

November

Su	Mo	Tu	We	Th	Fr	Sa
			1	2	3	4
5	6	7	8	9	10	11
12	13	14	15	16	17	18
19	20	21	22	23	24	25
26	27	28	29	30		

December

Su	Mo	Tu	We	Th	Fr	Sa
					1	2
3	4	5	6	7	8	9
10	11	12	13	14	15	16
17	18	19	20	21	22	23
24	25	26	27	28	29	30

"

THERE IS NO GREATER AGONY THAN BEARING AN UNTOLD STORY INSIDE YOU.

—Maya Angelou

TITLE OF MY BOOK

_____

BOOK TIMELINE

WEEK 1	WEEK 2	WEEK 3	WEEK 4
Research Topic	Research Topic	Research Topic	**Write!!!**
Write!!!	Plot/Theme	Target Audience	Research Topic
Plot/Theme	Outline	Outline	Book Length
Outline	**Write!!!**	Titles	Subtitles
Start Saving For	Titles	Brainstorm	Talking Point
Publishing	Brainstorm	Book Quotes	Brainstorm
Writing Goal		**Write!!!**	Authors
Brainstorm		Plot/Theme	

MONTH 1

WEEK 5	WEEK 6	WEEK 7	WEEK 8
Write!!!	Research Topic	Genre Research	Author Bio
Research Topic	Book Length	Target Audience	**Write!!!**
Subtitles	Graphics	Similar Books	Dedication
Start Saving	**Write!!!**	Word/Page Goal	Graphics
Brainstorm	Talking Point	Motivation	Authors
Plot/Theme	Questions	**Write!!!**	Talking Point
		Feedback	

MONTH 2

WEEK 9	WEEK 10	WEEK 11	WEEK 12
Write!!!	Cover Concept	Genre Research	Cover Concept
Formats/Fonts	Dedication	**Write!!!**	Marketing Tactics
Target Audience	Branding Ideas	Book Length	Branding Ideas
Acknowledgment	**Write!!!**	Acknowledgment	**Write!!!**
Book Quotes	Book Dimensions	2 publishers	Talking Point
Questions	Feedback	Word/Page Goal	

MONTH 3

WEEK 13	WEEK 14	WEEK 15	WEEK 16
Write!!!	Proofread Book	**Write!!!**	Proofread Book
Social Media	Social Media	Edit	Social Media
Cover Concept	Finalize Cover	Social Media	Author Bio
Description	Target Audience	Formats	TOC
Reviewers	Headshots	Branding Ideas	Index (If Applicable)
Launch Date	Quotes	Reviewers	Reviewers

MONTH 4

My Writing Goal:
It's important to set weekly writing goals to keep track of your ultimate word and page goal for your book. Use this to hold yourself accountable for your writing schedule.

_____

I Will Research:
Research is needed to collect information for and to go within your book. No matter the subject, you will need to conduct research to ensure you have correct and pertinent information.

_____

_____

The Initial Plot/ Theme Of My Book Is:
Take the idea from your head and put it on paper. When someone asks you, "What is your book about?" you'll be able to say this. Every week you will refine your answer until it's perfect.

_____

_____

My Book Publishing Contract Savings:
You should start saving for the publishing of your book. You may not have the exact price, but set a goal and stick to it.

_____

I Will Brainstorm About:
Research and writing aren't enough; You will also need to brainstorm new ideas and additions. This will help with research and beef up your book to reach its full potential.

_____

I Will Work On My Book Outline And:
You can always set additional weekly goals for yourself.

_____

MONDAY

Example: Decide exactly what it is I plan to write about.

TUESDAY

WEDNESDAY

THURSDAY

FRIDAY

SATURDAY

SUNDAY

NOTES

HELPFUL TIPS FOR WRITERS

01

If you're having writer's block, there are a few different things you can do to get some relief:

1. Go for a walk, or do something different to give your mind a break.
2. Eliminate distractions.
3. Change your environment.
4. Brainstorm ideas instead.
5. Have some coffee, take a small break.

02

Do you feel like you don't have enough time to write your book? Or, you're falling behind?

Maybe getting a ghostwriter is a good solution for you. Or, if you want to actually write your book yourself, then you can get creative with your opportunities to write. If you have a moment to yourself, then put notes in your phone.

03

Not sure what to write about? Or, want to refine your idea?

Start asking other people what they want to read about. Or, bounce ideas off of people. The best books are those answering questions that people actually have. Or, those that are providing information that does not exist yet. Think of new trends and concepts.

04

Have you written as much as you can, but it's not enough? Do you need more words on paper?

Then go back and explain things more thoroughly, add more details, and put more points or information to leave no room for questions. Asking others what they don't know about the topic can give you more insight into things to add to your book.

05

Are you having issues getting words from in your head onto the paper?

Try recording your book on a voice recorder. Any time you're thinking of things to put in your book, pull out your recorder and start talking away! Every cell phone is equipped with a voice recorder, so you already have one. Or, you can buy one of the more tradtional hand-held ones.

My Writing Goal:

_____

I Will Research:

_____

_____

The Refined Plot/Theme Of My Book Is:

_____

_____

My Book Publishing Contract Savings:

_____

I Will Brainstorm About:

_____

_____

I Will Work On My Book Outline, Titles, And:

_____

_____

_____

_____

WEEKLY GOALS

MONDAY

TUESDAY

WEDNESDAY

THURSDAY

FRIDAY

SATURDAY

SUNDAY

NOTES

COMMON WRITING MISTAKES

Subject-Verb Agreement

The subject and verb of a sentence must agree with one another in number whether they are singular or plural. If the subject of the sentence is singular, its verb must also be singular; and if the subject is plural, the verb must also be plural.

Sentence Fragments

Sentence fragments are incomplete sentences that don't have one independent clause. A fragment may lack a subject, a complete verb, or both. Sometimes fragments depend on the proceeding sentence to give it true meaning.

Comma Splice

A comma splice occurs when two separate sentences are joined with a comma rather than a period or semicolon. You can create comma splices when using transitional words, such as however, therefore, or moreover.

Vague Pronoun Reference

A pronoun can replace a noun, and its antecedent should be the person, place, or thing to which the pronoun refers. A vague pronoun reference (words such as it, that, this, and which) can leave the reader confused about what or to whom the pronoun refers.

Subject-Verb Agreement

A run-on sentence occurs when you connect two main clauses with no punctuation.

Sentence Fragments

A comma should always be after an introductory word, phrase, or clause. This actually gives the reader a slight pause after an introductory element and often can help avoid confusion.

My Writing Goal:

_____

I Will Research:

_____

_____

The Refined Plot/Theme Of My Book Is:

_____

_____

My Book Publishing Contract Savings:

_____

I Will Brainstorm About:

_____

_____

Motivational Quotes For Writing:
Collect quotes that you can refer to during your writing to inspire your writing when you need it.

_____

_____

I Will Work On My Book Outline, Titles, and:

_____

_____

WEEKLY GOALS

MONDAY

TUESDAY

WEDNESDAY

THURSDAY

FRIDAY

SATURDAY

SUNDAY

NOTES

QUESTIONS TO ASK YOURSELF

1. Why am I writing this book and what will it be used for?
2. What is the main theme?
3. What are the key principles?
4. What is my book about?
5. What do I want the reader to do as a result of reading my book?
6. How can this book help others?

My Writing Goal:

_____

I Will Research:

_____

_____

The Refined Plot/Theme Of My Book Is:

_____

_____

My Book Publishing Contract Savings:

_____

I Will Brainstorm About:

_____

_____

1 Talking Point About My Book:
You will need to be able to talk about your book in different aspects. Coming up with talking points will begin to prepare you for questions people may have about your book.

_____

_____

Authors That Inspire me:
List a few authors that inspire you to write, whether you love their book and/or style of writing. Studying other great writers will assist you with your writing and provide inspiration.

_____

_____

WEEKLY GOALS

MONDAY

TUESDAY

WEDNESDAY

THURSDAY

FRIDAY

SATURDAY

SUNDAY

NOTES

FIRST MONTH SAVINGS

$

My Writing Goal:

_____

I Will Research:

_____

_____

The Refined Plot/Theme Of My Book Is:

_____

_____

My Book Publishing Contract Savings:

_____

I Will Brainstorm About:

_____

_____

Some Of My Titles And Subtitles Are:

_____   _____

_____   _____

_____   _____

_____   _____

WEEKLY GOALS

MONDAY

TUESDAY

WEDNESDAY

THURSDAY

FRIDAY

SATURDAY

SUNDAY

NOTES

WRITING TIPS

READ

WRITE EVERY DAY

STOP WORRYING ABOUT BEING A GOOD WRITER; JUST WRITE.

DON'T BE A PERFECTIONIST

REMEMBER WHY YOU'RE WRITING

FIND YOUR RHYTHM AND WRITE.

My Writing Goal:

_____

I Will Research:

_____

_____

I Will Need Graphics Or Illustrations For:

Most books have graphics and illustrations inside of them. If you plan to have some inside of your book, you should start planning or thinking about the graphics you will need to be created.

_____

_____

My Book Publishing Contract Savings:

_____

Questions I need To Ask People For My Book:

Be sure to ask others what they want to know about the subject you're writing about. Doing so could provide insight and additional information for your book that it wouldn't have had otherwise.

_____

_____

1 Talking Point About My Book:

_____

_____

WEEKLY GOALS

MONDAY

TUESDAY

WEDNESDAY

THURSDAY

FRIDAY

SATURDAY

SUNDAY

NOTES

All books are either non-fiction or fiction. Non-fiction books contain factual information, such as biographies and history books. Fiction books contain a story which was made up by the author.

Science fiction	New Age
Satire	Encyclopedias
Drama	Dictionaries
Action and Adventure	Comics
Romance	Art
Mystery	Cookbooks
Horror	Diaries
Self help	Journals
Health	Prayer books
Guide	Series
Travel	Trilogy
Children's	Biographies
Science	Autobiographies
History	Fantasy
Math	Anthology
Religion	Poetry
Spirituality	

My Writing Goal:

_____

My Words/ Pages:

_____

Genres I Will Research For My Book To Fit In:

Research the categories your book will fall into. You are allowed to have up to 3. Having this information can help you stick to the topic at hand.

_____ _____

_____ _____

The Target Audience For My Book:

Every book is directed for certain people to read. When you identify those people, you can write specifically for and to them.

_____

_____

My Book Publishing Contract Savings:

_____

Books That Are Similar To Mine:

When you identify books that are similar to your topic, genre, and theme of your book, you can use them as a resource. You should take note of the style of writing, formatting, dimension, font, and anything else you like about the books.

_____

_____

The Things That Motivate Me To Write This Book:

Always keep in mind the things that inspire you to write this book. Doing so will provide you the momentum needed to continue on and complete it.

_____

I Will Ask For Feedback For My Book Idea.

WEEKLY GOALS

MONDAY

TUESDAY

WEDNESDAY

THURSDAY

FRIDAY

SATURDAY

SUNDAY

NOTES

WORD COUNT

It's important for every writer to have a word count goal for their book. Doing so will allow you to keep track of your writing timeline and ensure you're in the proper range for the type of book you're producing. Here are some basic word count guidelines you can follow, but keep in mind, these rules can sometimes change due to new trends.

10k Words → A pamphlet or business white paper.
Read time = 30-60 minutes.

20k Words → Short eBook. Read time: 1-2 hours.

40k-60k Words → Standard nonfiction book. Read time: 3-4 hours.

60k-80k Words → Long nonfiction book/standard-length novel. Read time: 4-6 hours.

80k-100k Words → Very long nonfiction book / long novel.

100k+ Words → Epic-length novel, academic book, biography. Read time:6-8 hours.

My Writing Goal:

_____

Authors That Motivate Me:
Identify authors to use their work as a reference for your book. You can improve your writing, develop a writing style, and use their works for inspiration and guidance.

_____   _____

_____   _____

Points To Put In My Author Bio:
You will need a biography as an author to inform people of who you are and why you are credible enough to write this book. It should include information about you and your career as it relates to your authorship.

_____

_____

My Book Publishing Contract Savings:

_____

I Am Dedicating My Book To:

_____

_____

Another Talking Point For My Book:
Continue to come up with more things to talk about regarding your book. By doing so, you'll sound more assured, always have a well-rounded response when being asked about your book, and find nifty ways to mention it in conversation.

_____

Graphics/Illustrations Needed:

_____

WEEKLY GOALS

MONDAY

TUESDAY

WEDNESDAY

THURSDAY

FRIDAY

SATURDAY

SUNDAY

NOTES

QUESTIONS TO ASK A PUBLISHER

1. What services do you provide—and who's doing the work?

2. Do you require exclusivity?

3. Is the fee structure transparent?

4. What royalties will I be paid?

5. Where will you distribute my book?

6. What will you do to market my book?

7. What is the timeline for publication?

8. How do I get out of the arrangement if it's not working for me?

9. What do you charge, how will you bill me and what are your terms?

10. What formats do you publish in?

11. Are there any bonuses in the contract when sales hit a certain target?

My Writing Goal:

_____

Book Publishing Savings:

_____

Fonts/Formats I like For My Book:

You will need to identify font combinations for your book. Books typically have different fonts for titles, subtitles, and content.

_____ _____

_____ _____

The Target Audience For My Book is:

_____

_____

My Book Acknowledgement Will Include:

You can acknowledge whomever you would like in your book. This portion is not required, but it is a way to thank those who have helped you or your book in any way.

_____

_____

Book Publishing Quotes:

You will need to begin contacting publishing companies, Like Opportune Publishing, to start requesting quotes for the publishing of your book. This will allow you to align your savings with your goals.

_____

Questions About My Book:

There will be times when someone will ask you questions aboutyour book. You should answer these within your book and prepare yourself to explain in person.

_____

_____

WEEKLY GOALS

MONDAY

TUESDAY

WEDNESDAY

THURSDAY

FRIDAY

SATURDAY

SUNDAY

NOTES

FONT COMBOS

No matter how stunning your book cover is, or how amazing the story, choosing the right font for your book can make a big difference when you publish your book. Creating a coherent and visually correct reading flow is important. The key is not to distract, but instead, help the reader concentrate on the content.

Bembo (body)
IDDragonXing (Chapter)

ONE

Minion Pro (body)
Aaargh (Chapter)

CHAPTER

ONE

Garamond Premier Pro (body)
Steelfish (Chapter)

CHAPTER ONE

Sabon (body)
Quicksand (Chapter)

Chapter Title   1

Sabon (body)
Humanst521LtEU (Chapter)

CHAPTER ONE

rescuing the princess

Dante MT (body)
Amor Sans (Chapter),
Bickham Script (Dropcap)

CHAPTER

ONE

OTHER FONTS

Tryst AaBbCcDdEeFfGgHhIiJ   Cardo AaBbCcDdEeFfGgHhIiJjK

Theano Didot AaBbCcDdEeFfGgH   EB Garamond AaBbCcDdEeFfG

My Writing Goal:

_____

My Book Cover Concept:
You should begin thinking about how you would like your book to look.
Describe your front and back cover ideas.

_____

_____

My Book Publishing Contract Savings:

_____

Some Of My Branding Ideas For My Books:
Every book and author should have its own brand in order to market
successfully. This will set the tone for you and your book and how you both
should be viewed. Branding can include colors, fonts, image styles, etc

_____

_____

_____

Book Dimensions I Want My Book To Be:
Thinking of the size that your book will be can help you visualize your book.
Use other books as a reference.

_____   _____

The Feedback I've Gotten For My Book:
Telling people about your book will open it up to feedback and allow you to
think of things you wouldn't have otherwise. Use this information to edit and
alter your book going forward.

_____

_____

_____

WEEKLY GOALS

MONDAY

TUESDAY

WEDNESDAY

THURSDAY

FRIDAY

SATURDAY

SUNDAY

NOTES

BOOK PUBLISHING SERVICES

COPYEDITING

COPYWRITING

MARKETING MATERIALS

BOOK REVIEW SERVICE

MULTI-LANGUAGE

EBOOK PUBLISHING

BOOK FORMATTING

BOOK COVER DESIGN

ISBN ASSIGNMENT

BARCODES

COPYRIGHT

DISTRIBUTION LIST

ILLUSTRATIONS

GRAPHIC DESIGN

GHOSTWRITING

My Writing Goal:

_____

Book Genres I Like For My Book:

_____   _____

_____   _____

My Book Publishing Contract Savings:

_____

The Book Length I Would Like My Book To Be:
You should determine how long you would like your book to be. The length can sometimes determine the category.

_____

People I Want To Acknowledge In My Book:

_____   _____

_____   _____

2 Publishing Companies I Like:

_____

My Page And Word Count Goals For My Book:

_____   _____

WEEKLY GOALS

WEEK 11 OF 16

MONDAY

TUESDAY

WEDNESDAY

THURSDAY

FRIDAY

SATURDAY

SUNDAY

NOTES

HELLO! I AM

An Author

My Writing Goal:

_____

The Cover Concept For My Book:

_____

_____

My Book Publishing Contract Savings:

_____

Marketing Tactics I Want To Use For My Book:
The essential part of selling books is the marketing done for it. This will allow your book to be exposed in ways it wouldn't have otherwise and drive sales.

_____

_____

Some Branding Ideas For My Book And Me:

_____

_____

More Talking Points About My Book:

_____

_____

_____

_____

WEEKLY GOALS

MONDAY

TUESDAY

WEDNESDAY

THURSDAY

FRIDAY

SATURDAY

SUNDAY

NOTES

IMPROVE YOUR WRITING VOCABULARY

USE NEW WORDS	READ EVERY DAY	MAKE WORD LIST	USE MNEMONICS
USE A THESAURUS	VOCABULARY WORDBOOKS	LEARN NEW WORDS	STUDY VOCABULARY
DO WORD PUZZLES	KEEP A JOURNAL	USE A DICTIONARY	DIVERSIFY YOUR READING LIST

My Writing Goal:

_____

The Cover Concept For My Book:

_____

_____

My Book Publishing Contract Savings:

_____

Begin Social Media Debut By:

One of the most vital tactics for marketing your book will be through social media exposure. You can begin with making social media pages and posts to serve as a teaser for your book.

_____

_____

My Book Description Will Include:

_____

_____

Identify Book Reviewers:

Allowing key people to read your book will give you honest feedback on your writing. Doing so at an early stage will provide you with the opportunity to make last minute changes and see what others would think. You could use these as advanced reviews to post or display for advertising as well.

_____

_____

My Ideal Book Launch Date:

Choose an ideal launch date to serve as a deadline and schedule to have writing finalized and savings goals met. The time is tentative until finalized with the publisher.

_____

WEEKLY GOALS

MONDAY

TUESDAY

WEDNESDAY

THURSDAY

FRIDAY

SATURDAY

SUNDAY

NOTES

TRADITIONAL TRIM SIZES

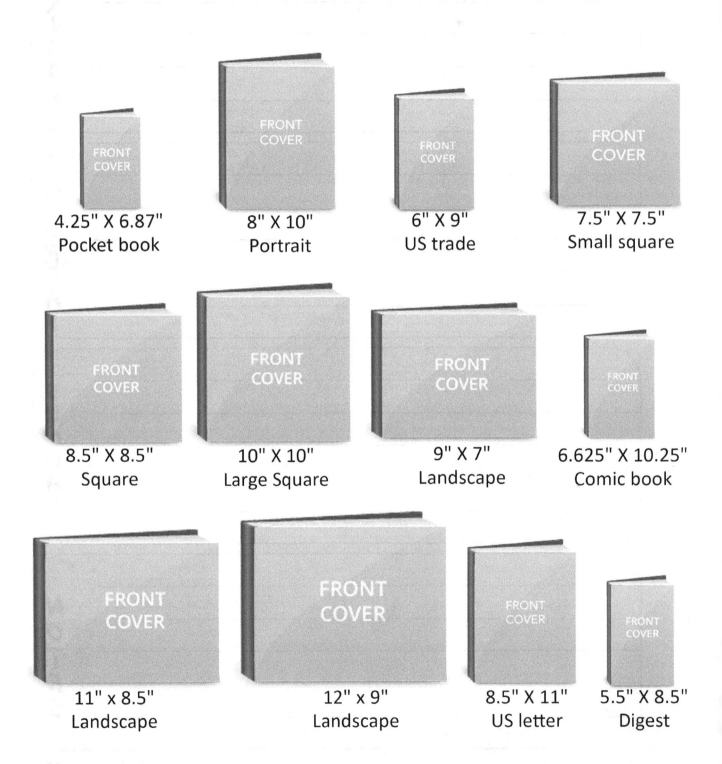

4.25" X 6.87"
Pocket book

8" X 10"
Portrait

6" X 9"
US trade

7.5" X 7.5"
Small square

8.5" X 8.5"
Square

10" X 10"
Large Square

9" X 7"
Landscape

6.625" X 10.25"
Comic book

11" x 8.5"
Landscape

12" x 9"
Landscape

8.5" X 11"
US letter

5.5" X 8.5"
Digest

My Writing Goal:

_____

The Cover Concept For My Book:

_____

_____

My Book Publishing Contract Savings:

_____

Get Professional Headshots Done.
You'll need to have professional headshots done for marketing materials, social media, and online book profiles. Being an author is a profession, so you must have professional photos.

Proof Read My Book.

Book Publishing Quotes:

_____   _____

_____   _____

Some Social Media Posts I Will Create:

_____

_____

_____

WEEKLY GOALS

MONDAY

TUESDAY

WEDNESDAY

THURSDAY

FRIDAY

SATURDAY

SUNDAY

NOTES

"

YOU MUST STAY DRUNK ON WRITING SO REALITY CANNOT DESTROY YOU.

– Ray Bradbury

My Writing Goal:

_____

Book Formats I Want My Book In:

_____

_____

My Book Publishing Contract Savings:

_____

Edit My Book.

Some Social Media Posts I Will Create:

_____

_____

_____

I Plan To Brand My Book And Myself As:

_____

_____

The Reviewers I Will Send My Book To:

_____   _____

_____   _____

WEEKLY GOALS

MONDAY

TUESDAY

WEDNESDAY

THURSDAY

FRIDAY

SATURDAY

SUNDAY

NOTES

BOOK BINDING OPTIONS

ADHESIVE CASE WRAP AND DUST JACKET

ADHESIVE CASE WRAP

BLACK COMB

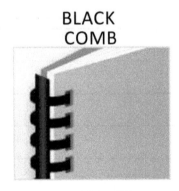

BLACK SPIRAL

SADDLE STITCHING

PERFECT BINDING

I Will Proof Read My Book.

My Book Publishing Contract Savings:

_____

Some Social Media Posts I Will Create:

_____

_____

_____

Gather Chapters To Build The Table Of Contents.

Collect Words To Compile For The Index And/Or Glossary (If Applicable).

Finalize These Things:

- [ ] Book Descriptions
- [ ] Acknowledgements
- [ ] Description
- [ ] Cover Concept
- [ ] 3 Talking Points
- [ ] Titles And Subtitles
- [ ] Author Bio
- [ ] Book Dimensions

WEEKLY GOALS

MONDAY

TUESDAY

WEDNESDAY

THURSDAY

FRIDAY

SATURDAY

SUNDAY

NOTES

CREATE AN AUTHOR WEBSITE

Your site should be a marketing tool that serves as the hub of all your online activity, from blogging to selling books to emailing a newsletter to participating in social media. Use a platform like WordPress, Squarespace, or Wix to build a site easily.

SET UP A BLOG ON YOUR SITE

Provide a "behind the scenes look" for readers by blogging once or twice a month. Fans will love the insight into your personality and writing process, and anything you post is fodder for your next email to subscribers.

LINK TO YOUR PUBLISHED BOOKS

Create a site page linking to your books to make it easy for readers to discover all the titles you've written. Include cover images, brief elevator pitches, and links to multiple retailers so readers can purchase your books wherever they shop.

BUILD A MAILING LIST ON YOUR SITE

Include a simple form on your homepage, website pages, and/or blog's sidebar asking for visitors' email addresses. Collecting email addresses lets you build relationships with people who want to hear from you.

WELCOME VISITORS WITH AN EMAIL AUTO RESPONSE

When people subscribe to updates from you via your website, send them a welcome email including either a link to a permafree ebook, sample chapters, or some sort of freebie as a "thank you" for signing up.

CLAIM YOUR BOOKBUB AUTHOR PROFILE

Make sure your BookBub Author Profile is up to date so fans and potential readers can learn more about you and your books.

GET MORE BOOKBUB FOLLOWERS

The more followers you have, the more people will receive dedicated emails from BookBub notifying them about your new releases and price promotions. And once you get 1K followers, you can also send BookBub Preorder Alerts!

ADD A BOOKBUB FOLLOW BUTTON TO YOUR SITE

Make sure website visitors can find your BookBub Author Profile by adding a follow button or icon to your site, wherever it fits best into the site design.

CLAIM YOUR SOCIAL MEDIA PROFILES

Grab your username on Facebook, Twitter, Instagram, Pinterest, Tumblr, Google+, LinkedIn, and About.me. Even if you don't have active profiles on each site, at least claim your name and direct people who visit to your most active social media profile instead.

LINK YOUR WEBSITE AND AUTHOR PROFILE

Once you've created a website and claimed your BookBub Author Profile, make sure that people can find these assets by linking to them on your email signature and bio sections on your social media profiles.

CREATE A VIDEO BLOG

Upload videos to YouTube and embed each video in a blog post. In these videos, you can answer fan questions, partner with another author to interview each other, list book recommendations, or do a short reading from an upcoming new release. Experiment with a few simple videos to see if you're comfortable vlogging before focusing on production quality.

CONGRATULATIONS!!

You have now written your first (or next) book. I knew you could do it! All you needed was a little momentum, determination and the *Book Writing Guide*.

It's now time to move on to publishing your masterpiece. You can go to **www.bookwritingguide.com/Publish** to get your free e-book on what to do after you have written your book. There you will find a helpful, short but sweet guide for your burning question— *I've written my book, now what's next?*

Since your book is a proven success from the *Book Writing Guide*, you can have it absolutely **FREE!** All you have to do is add it to your cart and checkout using this **coupon code: BWG423** to gain access to the next steps toward authorship.

You are truly appreciated, and I thank you for trusting this awesome guide to assist you in writing your book!

If you're looking for a publisher, contact Opportune Publishing for answers to questions, quotes, and book publishing services.

www.opportunepublishing.com
(832) 263-1700

I AM READY TO WRITE MY NEXT BOOK

TITLE OF MY BOOK

_____

BOOK TIMELINE

	WEEK 1	WEEK 2	WEEK 3	WEEK 4
MONTH 1	Research Topic **Write!!!** Plot/Theme Outline Start Saving For Publishing Writing Goal Brainstorm	Research Topic Plot/Theme Outline **Write!!!** Titles Brainstorm	Research Topic Target Audience Outline Titles Brainstorm Book Quotes **Write!!!** Plot/Theme	**Write!!!** Research Topic Book Length Subtitles Talking Point Brainstorm Authors

	WEEK 5	WEEK 6	WEEK 7	WEEK 8
MONTH 2	**Write!!!** Research Topic Subtitles Start Saving Brainstorm Plot/Theme	Research Topic Book Length Graphics **Write!!!** Talking Point Questions	Genre Research Target Audience Similar Books Word/Page Goal Motivation **Write!!!** Feedback	Author Bio **Write!!!** Dedication Graphics Authors Talking Point

	WEEK 9	WEEK 10	WEEK 11	WEEK 12
MONTH 3	**Write!!!** Formats/Fonts Target Audience Acknowledgment Book Quotes Questions	Cover Concept Dedication Branding Ideas **Write!!!** Book Dimensions Feedback	Genre Research **Write!!!** Book Length Acknowledgment 2 publishers Word/Page Goal	Cover Concept Marketing Tactics Branding Ideas **Write!!!** Talking Point

	WEEK 13	WEEK 14	WEEK 15	WEEK 16
MONTH 4	**Write!!!** Social Media Cover Concept Description Reviewers Launch Date	Proofread Book Social Media Finalize Cover Target Audience Headshots Quotes	**Write!!!** Edit Social Media Formats Branding Ideas Reviewers	Proofread Book Social Media Author Bio TOC Index (If Applicable) Reviewers

My Writing Goal:
It's important to set weekly writing goals to keep track of your ultimate word and page goal for your book. Use this to hold yourself accountable for your writing schedule.

_____

I Will Research:
Research is needed to collect information for and to go within your book. No matter the subject, you will need to conduct research to ensure you have correct and pertinent information.

_____

_____

The Initial Plot/ Theme Of My Book Is:
Take the idea from your head and put it on paper. When someone asks you, "What is your book about?" you'll be able to say this. Every week you will refine your answer until it's perfect.

_____

_____

My Book Publishing Contract Savings:
You should start saving for the publishing of your book. You may not have the exact price, but set a goal and stick to it.

_____

I Will Brainstorm About:
Research and writing aren't enough; You will also need to brainstorm new ideas and additions. This will help with research and beef up your book to reach its full potential.

_____

I Will Work On My Book Outline And:
You can always set additional weekly goals for yourself.

_____

WEEKLY GOALS

MONDAY

TUESDAY

WEDNESDAY

THURSDAY

FRIDAY

SATURDAY

SUNDAY

NOTES

"

PERFECTION IS NOT ATTAINABLE, BUT IF WE CHASE PERFECTION WE CAN CATCH EXCELLENCE."

—Vince Lombardi

My Writing Goal:

_____

I Will Research:

_____

_____

The Refined Plot/Theme Of My Book Is:

_____

_____

My Book Publishing Contract Savings:

_____

I Will Brainstorm About:

_____

_____

I Will Work On My Book Outline, Titles, And:

_____

_____

_____

_____

WEEKLY GOALS

MONDAY

TUESDAY

WEDNESDAY

THURSDAY

FRIDAY

SATURDAY

SUNDAY

NOTES

"

A PERSON WHO NEVER MADE A MISTAKE NEVER TRIED ANYTHING NEW.

–Albert Einstein

My Writing Goal:

_____

I Will Research:

_____

_____

The Refined Plot/Theme Of My Book Is:

_____

_____

My Book Publishing Contract Savings:

_____

I Will Brainstorm About:

_____

_____

Motivational Quotes For Writing:
Collect quotes that you can refer to during your writing to inspire your writing when you need it.

_____

_____

I Will Work On My Book Outline, Titles, and:

_____

_____

WEEKLY GOALS

MONDAY

TUESDAY

WEDNESDAY

THURSDAY

FRIDAY

SATURDAY

SUNDAY

NOTES

1 BOOK DOWN, 1 TO GO.

My Writing Goal:

_____

I Will Research:

_____

_____

The Refined Plot/Theme Of My Book Is:

_____

_____

My Book Publishing Contract Savings:

_____

I Will Brainstorm About:

_____

_____

1 Talking Point About My Book:

You will need to be able to talk about your book in different aspects. Coming up with talking points will begin to prepare you for questions people may have about your book.

_____

_____

Authors That Inspire me:

List a few authors that inspire you to write, whether you love their book and/or style of writing. Studying other great writers will assist you with your writing and provide inspiration.

_____

_____

WEEKLY GOALS

MONDAY

TUESDAY

WEDNESDAY

THURSDAY

FRIDAY

SATURDAY

SUNDAY

NOTES

"

___

IF THERE'S A BOOK THAT YOU WANT TO READ, BUT IT HASN'T BEEN WRITTEN YET, THEN YOU MUST WRITE IT.

___

—Toni Morrison

My Writing Goal:

_____

I Will Research:

_____

_____

The Refined Plot/Theme Of My Book Is:

_____

_____

My Book Publishing Contract Savings:

_____

I Will Brainstorm About:

_____

_____

Some Of My Titles And Subtitles Are:

_____   _____

_____   _____

_____   _____

_____   _____

_____   _____

WEEKLY GOALS

MONDAY

TUESDAY

WEDNESDAY

THURSDAY

FRIDAY

SATURDAY

SUNDAY

NOTES

"

WHAT WE ACHIEVE IN WARDLY WILL CHANGE OUTER REALITY.

—Plutarch

My Writing Goal:

_____

I Will Research:

_____

_____

I Will Need Graphics Or Illustrations For:
Most books have graphics and illustrations inside of them. If you plan to have some inside of your book, you should start planning or thinking about the graphics you will need to be created.

_____

_____

My Book Publishing Contract Savings:

_____

Questions I need To Ask People For My Book:
Be sure to ask others what they want to know about the subject you're writing about. Doing so could provide insight and additional information for your book that it wouldn't have had otherwise.

_____

_____

1 Talking Point About My Book:

_____

_____

WEEKLY GOALS

MONDAY

TUESDAY

WEDNESDAY

THURSDAY

FRIDAY

SATURDAY

SUNDAY

NOTES

"

CHANGE YOUR THOUGHTS
AND YOU CHANGE YOUR WORLD

—Norman Vincent Peale

My Writing Goal: My Words/ Pages:

_____   _____

Genres I Will Research For My Book To Fit In:
Research the categories your book will fall into. You are allowed to have up to 3. Having this information can help you stick to the topic at hand.

_____   _____

_____   _____

The Target Audience For My Book:
Every book is directed for certain people to read. When you identify those people, you can write specifically for and to them.

_____

_____

My Book Publishing Contract Savings:

_____

Books That Are Similar To Mine:
When you identify books that are similar to your topic, genre, and theme of your book, you can use them as a resource. You should take note of the style of writing, formatting, dimension, font, and anything else you like about the books.

_____

_____

The Things That Motivate Me To Write This Book:
Always keep in mind the things that inspire you to write this book. Doing so will provide you the momentum needed to continue on and complete it.

_____

I Will Ask For Feedback For My Book Idea.

WEEKLY GOALS

MONDAY

TUESDAY

WEDNESDAY

THURSDAY

FRIDAY

SATURDAY

SUNDAY

NOTES

"

SETTING GOALS IS THE FIRST STEP IN TURNING THE INVISIBLE INTO THE VISIBLE.

–Tony Robbins

My Writing Goal:

_____

Authors That Motivate Me:
Identify authors to use their work as a reference for your book. You can improve your writing, develop a writing style, and use their works for inspiration and guidance.

_____   _____

_____   _____

Points To Put In My Author Bio:
You will need a biography as an author to inform people of who you are and why you are credible enough to write this book. It should include information about you and your career as it relates to your authorship.

_____

_____

My Book Publishing Contract Savings:

_____

I Am Dedicating My Book To:

_____

_____

Another Talking Point For My Book:
Continue to come up with more things to talk about regarding your book. By doing so, you'll sound more assured, always have a well-rounded response when being asked about your book, and find nifty ways to mention it in conversation.

_____

Graphics/Illustrations Needed:

_____

WEEKLY GOALS

MONDAY

TUESDAY

WEDNESDAY

THURSDAY

FRIDAY

SATURDAY

SUNDAY

NOTES

KEEP WRITING!

My Writing Goal:

Book Publishing Savings:

_____

_____

Fonts/Formats I like For My Book:

You will need to identify font combinations for your book. Books typically have different fonts for titles, subtitles, and content.

_____   _____

_____   _____

The Target Audience For My Book is:

_____

_____

My Book Acknowledgement Will Include:

You can acknowledge whomever you would like in your book. This portion is not required, but it is a way to thank those who have helped you or your book in any way.

_____

_____

Book Publishing Quotes:

You will need to begin contacting publishing companies, Like Opportune Publishing, to start requesting quotes for the publishing of your book. This will allow you to align your savings with your goals.

_____

Questions About My Book:

There will be times when someone will ask you questions aboutyour book. You should answer these within your book and prepare yourself to explain in person.

_____

_____

WEEKLY GOALS

MONDAY

TUESDAY

WEDNESDAY

THURSDAY

FRIDAY

SATURDAY

SUNDAY

NOTES

"

BELIEVE YOU CAN AND YOU'RE HALFWAY THERE.

—Theodore Roosevelt

My Writing Goal:

_____

My Book Cover Concept:
You should begin thinking about how you would like your book to look.
Describe your front and back cover ideas.

_____

_____

My Book Publishing Contract Savings:

_____

Some Of My Branding Ideas For My Books:
Every book and author should have its own brand in order to market
successfully. This will set the tone for you and your book and how you both
should be viewed. Branding can include colors, fonts, image styles, etc

_____

_____

_____

Book Dimensions I Want My Book To Be:
Thinking of the size that your book will be can help you visualize your book.
Use other books as a reference.

_____   _____

The Feedback I've Gotten For My Book:
Telling people about your book will open it up to feedback and allow you to
think of things you wouldn't have otherwise. Use this information to edit and
alter your book going forward.

_____

_____

_____

WEEKLY GOALS

MONDAY

TUESDAY

WEDNESDAY

THURSDAY

FRIDAY

SATURDAY

SUNDAY

NOTES

"

TOO MANY OF US ARE NOT LIVING OUR DREAMS BECAUSE WE ARE LIVING OUR FEARS.

–Les Brown

My Writing Goal:

_____

Book Genres I Like For My Book:

_____   _____

_____   _____

My Book Publishing Contract Savings:

_____

The Book Length I Would Like My Book To Be:
You should determine how long you would like your book to be. The length can sometimes determine the category.

_____

People I Want To Acknowledge In My Book:

_____   _____

_____   _____

2 Publishing Companies I Like:

_____

My Page And Word Count Goals For My Book:

_____   _____

WEEKLY GOALS

MONDAY

TUESDAY

WEDNESDAY

THURSDAY

FRIDAY

SATURDAY

SUNDAY

NOTES

"

SET YOUR GOALS HIGH, AND DON'T STOP TILL YOU GET THERE.

—Bo Jackson

My Writing Goal:

_____

The Cover Concept For My Book:

_____

_____

My Book Publishing Contract Savings:

_____

Marketing Tactics I Want To Use For My Book:
The essential part of selling books is the marketing done for it. This will allow your book to be exposed in ways it wouldn't have otherwise and drive sales.

_____

_____

Some Branding Ideas For My Book And Me:

_____

_____

More Talking Points About My Book:

_____

_____

_____

_____

WEEKLY GOALS

MONDAY

TUESDAY

WEDNESDAY

THURSDAY

FRIDAY

SATURDAY

SUNDAY

NOTES

"

YOU CAN'T USE UP CREATIVITY. THE MORE YOU USE, THE MORE YOU HAVE

–Maya Angelou

My Writing Goal:

_____

The Cover Concept For My Book:

_____

_____

My Book Publishing Contract Savings:

_____

Begin Social Media Debut By:
One of the most vital tactics for marketing your book will be through social media exposure. You can begin with making social media pages and posts to serve as a teaser for your book.

_____

_____

My Book Description Will Include:

_____

_____

Identify Book Reviewers:
Allowing key people to read your book will give you honest feedback on your writing. Doing so at an early stage will provide you with the opportunity to make last minute changes and see what others would think. You could use these as advanced reviews to post or display for advertising as well.

_____

_____

My Ideal Book Launch Date:
Choose an ideal launch date to serve as a deadline and schedule to have writing finalized and savings goals met. The time is tentative until finalized with the publisher.

_____

WEEKLY GOALS

MONDAY

TUESDAY

WEDNESDAY

THURSDAY

FRIDAY

SATURDAY

SUNDAY

NOTES

"

PEOPLE WITH GOALS SUCCEED BECAUSE THEY KNOW WHERE THEY'RE GOING.

–Earl Nightingale

My Writing Goal:

_____

The Cover Concept For My Book:

_____

_____

My Book Publishing Contract Savings:

_____

Get Professional Headshots Done.
You'll need to have professional headshots done for marketing materials, social media, and online book profiles. Being an author is a profession, so you must have professional photos.

Proof Read My Book.

Book Publishing Quotes:

_____   _____

_____   _____

Some Social Media Posts I Will Create:

_____

_____

_____

WEEKLY GOALS

MONDAY

TUESDAY

WEDNESDAY

THURSDAY

FRIDAY

SATURDAY

SUNDAY

NOTES

 **WRITE 1ST BOOK**

 **WRITE 2ND BOOK**

 BUY ANOTHER BOOK WRITING GUIDE

WWW.BOOKWRITINGGUIDE.COM

My Writing Goal:

_____

Book Formats I Want My Book In:

_____

_____

My Book Publishing Contract Savings:

_____

Edit My Book.

Some Social Media Posts I Will Create:

_____

_____

_____

I Plan To Brand My Book And Myself As:

_____

_____

The Reviewers I Will Send My Book To:

_____   _____

_____   _____

WEEKLY GOALS

MONDAY

TUESDAY

WEDNESDAY

THURSDAY

FRIDAY

SATURDAY

SUNDAY

NOTES

"

ONE WAY TO KEEP MOMENTUM GOING IS TO HAVE CONSTANTLY GREATER GOALS.

—Michael Korda

I Will Proof Read My Book.

My Book Publishing Contract Savings:

_____

Some Social Media Posts I Will Create:

_____

_____

_____

Gather Chapters To Build The Table Of Contents.

Collect Words To Compile For The Index And/Or Glossary (If Applicable).

Finalize These Things:
- ☐ Book Descriptions
- ☐ Acknowledgements
- ☐ Description
- ☐ Cover Concept
- ☐ 3 Talking Points
- ☐ Titles And Subtitles
- ☐ Author Bio
- ☐ Book Dimensions

WEEKLY GOALS

MONDAY

TUESDAY

WEDNESDAY

THURSDAY

FRIDAY

SATURDAY

SUNDAY

NOTES